D0604231

Food For Good Health

DIGESTION: FOOD AT WORK

Barbara J. Patten, MS

The Rourke Corporation, Inc.
Vero Beach, Florida 32964

PHOTO CREDITS
All photos © Barbara and John Patten

Library of Congress Cataloging-in-Publication Data

Patten, Barbara J., 1951-
      Digestion: food at work / Barbara J. Patten.
      p. cm. — (Food for good health)
      Includes index.
      Summary: Briefly describes the parts of the digestive system and explains how they process the food we eat.
      ISBN 0-86593-403-7
      1. Digestion—Juvenile literature. [1. Digestive system.
2. Digestion.] I. Title. II. Series.
QP145.P18   1996
612.3—dc20   95-33537
                                                           CIP
                                                           AC

Printed in the USA

TABLE OF CONTENTS

DIGESTION OF FOOD

Hello teeth —
Hang on gums —
Wake up stomach —
Here it comes!

This poem sounds funny, but it is good science. In fact, it's a great start to the story of what happens to the food we eat.

Grab a banana and take a seat. Let's read all about how food in our bodies is digested and used.

Grab a banana and find out how
the body uses food.

DIGESTION AT WORK

Digestion (dii JES chun) is an important body function. It's what happens to food after people eat it.

Digestion frees **nutrients** (NOO tree ents), or chemicals that help the body work and grow, that are in good foods we eat. It releases all of the power in food for our bodies to use.

Digestion turns food into something the body can use.

Teeth start the digestion process by chewing food into small bits.

The digestive system includes the mouth, teeth, **esophagus** (ee SOF ah gus), stomach, and the small and large intestines.

Digestion breaks down food into tiny, tiny bits. These bits feed each of the billions of **cells** (SELZ) that make up the human body.

THE ESOPHAGUS

The esophagus begins at the back of your mouth. It is a tube that connects your mouth and throat with your stomach.

When you swallow, muscles in the esophagus push the chewed food down into the stomach.

Your esophagus and windpipe are set up so food doesn't "go down the wrong pipe" into the lungs. When you swallow, a flap of skin called the **epiglottis** (ep i GLAHT is) covers the windpipe to keep food out.

The giraffe has a long esophagus.

THE STOMACH

Food is churned, or mixed around, in the stomach by strong muscles. The food mixes with digestive acids called **gastric juices** (GAS trik JOO sez).

Gastric juices break down protein foods like meats, eggs and milk to release nutrients.

Food stays in the stomach for two to five hours, depending on how easy it is to break down. When food mixes with gastric juices, it becomes a thick liquid called **chyme** (KIIM).

Stomach muscles mix food with digestive acids.

THE SMALL INTESTINE

This part of the digestive system is located below the stomach.

Small intestines in an adult really aren't that small. The small intestine is about 20 feet long when it is unfolded.

The small intestine is below the stomach.

Foods like these are broken down in the small intestine, too.

The chyme goes from the stomach into the small intestine. Digestion is completed there. Juices from the small intestine walls break down chyme even more.

Also, the small intestine breaks down fats, another body nutrient, into bits our bodies can use.

INTO THE BLOODSTREAM

As digestion is completed, useful nutrients pass right through the walls of the small intestine into the blood.

The blood carries its fresh supply of nutrients to every cell. Cells get the nourishment they need as this food-rich blood flows by.

Cells take the nutrients from the blood as it goes through the body. Then, the blood moves past the small intestine again, and picks up a new food supply.

Blood carries digested food to every cell,
so you'll have energy to swim and play.

THE LARGE INTESTINE

Some parts of the foods we eat don't digest. They stay too large to pass through the wall of the small intestine and into the bloodstream. They move out of the end of the small intestine into the large intestine.

This undigested food, called body waste, can't be used. Our bodies get rid of body waste when we go to the bathroom.

Peanut shells cannot be digested.

DIGESTION NEVER STOPS

Eating is something people choose to do. They can pick the foods they want to eat, and when they want to eat them.

Digestion, however, is not like eating—or like running or talking. We never have to think about digestion. It takes place all by itself, automatically.

Sailors digest lunch as they float along.

Dogs don't have to think about digestion either.

Digestion is an **involuntary** (in VAHL uhn tayr ee) process, something that people can't start or stop. It goes on like the beating of your heart.

Digestion is amazing. It goes on day and night without stopping while we work, play and sleep.

EAT RIGHT AND GROW STRONG

Learn about digestion and you find out a lot of things about food. It's simple. Your body uses the best and throws out the rest.

Be good at choosing your food. Put the right kinds of foods in your mouth and chew. That's all you have to do.

You and your amazing body are a powerful team. Your body won't let your team down. Can you do the same?

Your body uses the best and gets rid of the rest.

GLOSSARY

cells (SELZ) — the smallest living part of any living thing

chyme (KIIM) — a thick liquid made from food mixed with gastric juices

digestion (dii JES chun) — what happens to food after people eat it

epiglottis (ep i GLAHT is) — a flap of skin that closes over the windpipe to keep food out of the lungs

esophagus (ee SOF ah gus) — tube that connects the mouth and throat to the stomach

gastric juices (GAS trik JOO sez) — digestive stomach acids

involuntary (in VAHL un tayr ee) — something that people can't start or stop

nutrients (NOO tree ents) — chemicals in food the body uses to work and grow

You and your body can be a good team.

INDEX